The Management Map II...

Companion Workbook

Deborah Avrin, MS, SPHR

ManageSmart Publishing

Published by ManageSmart Publishing
Plano, Texas
972-881-5282

Printed in the United States of America

ISBN: 978-0-9820901-3-8

Cover design: MC2 Graphics

To Stuart Avrin, my beloved husband who put up with all my crazy ideas.

Contents

Acknowledgments

The activities in *The Management Map II...Companion Workbook* looked great to me but the question is, would the activities work great when someone else was facilitating the material?

Three volunteers completed a field test and I was excited that each was from a different industry. Without their ideas, willingness to contribute, and tough love, the birth of *The Management Map II Companion Workbook* would not have been possible. I gratefully acknowledge the contributions of Amber James in the legal sector, Deborah Lief in the healthcare industry, and Judy Martin in the manufacturing industry, for their feedback. Judy Martin took the field test to a new level when she asked each of her participants to facilitate a chapter, proving that managers could facilitate the material with other managers. Judy has been involved since the first *Management Map* and words can't express how appreciative I am to have had her on this journey with me.

Carol Glynn, my book accountability buddy when I wrote *The Management Map II...Navigation Tools for Managers Transitioning to Leadership*, again offered her support and encouragement throughout this process. Setting goals and deadlines with Carol encouraged me to create this last tool in *The Management Map* series.

Since this is the last book in the series, I reflected back on the start of this journey in 2008. I would like to acknowledge two friends who, because they both wrote a book, gave me the confidence that I could also author my own. Thank you to Sharon Redd and Carl Youngberg for your inspiration and encouragement.

A terrific team of professionals also contributed to the successful completion of this book: cover designer Alan McCuller, who created a theme design that could be used throughout *The Management Map* series, and editor Martha McCuller.

Finally, I am so grateful to my family and friends who always encourage me to follow my dreams, especially my husband, Stuart Avrin.

Introduction

Many people keep a travel journal when they go on a journey. The purpose of a travel journal is to record experiences and preserve memories. Travelers realize their journey is about what they are seeing and hearing and also about what they are thinking and feeling. A natural follow-up to the book *The Management Map II...Navigation Tools for Managers Transitioning to Leadership* is this *Companion Workbook*, which serves as your travel journal during your management journey.

After you read each chapter in *The Management Map II*, turn to the matching section in the *Companion Workbook*. Each section begins with a list of items to collect before beginning the activities and a summary of the chapter to provide you with a refresher of key concepts. Allow about one to one and a half hours to complete the activities for each chapter. Each session begins with the following reflective questions to refresh your memory about the chapter content and prepare you for a deeper dive in the concepts through the learning activities:
- What did you like best about the chapter? What topic resonated with you?
- Which concepts in the chapter apply to your department or organization?
- Which quote did you like from the chapter?

The activities in the chapter are listed under "Journey Progress" for you to check when completed. The workbook contains 50 activities. You can complete all the activities or just pick and choose those most relevant for your position. Some activities are designed for you to try on-the-job by interviewing an employee or leading a brainstorming session. These activities are designated by the code "OTJ" in the table of contents. Be sure to note the reference pages to review in *The Management Map II...Navigation Tools for Managers Transitioning to Leadership* before you begin each activity.

Suggested uses for this book include:
- **Self-study** — For managers who prefer to learn on their own. You can reflect on the concepts alone or locate a coach or accountability partner to provide you with someone to discuss ideas and concepts.
- **Coaching** — *The Management Map II* and its *Companion Workbook* are great tools for coaching managers one-on-one. Simply assign chapters and then conduct your coaching sessions around the concepts and how specifically to apply them in their positions.
- **Self-directed study groups** — A study group at work can act like a book club. Locate a small group of people who are in similar job positions and create a meeting schedule. Group members can take turns facilitating activities during the sessions.
- **Facilitator-led workshops** — Facilitators can schedule sessions for participants and use the *Companion Workbook* in a workshop setting. You can customize the learning experience by adding your company's philosophy, policies, and procedures to the activities. The activities in the workbook are designed for managers to embark on a journey of self-discovery. Participants learn by doing, not lecture.

The act of writing things down helps reinforce concepts and adds them to your long term memory. Using **The Management Map II Companion Workbook** will increase your retention of the knowledge and skills you are gaining.

Enjoy your management journey and your new travel journal.

ONE

ON THE ROAD AGAIN...
Advanced Management Mapping

Items to Collect for This Chapter's Activities:
❑ Your organization's vision statement
❑ Your organization's list of core competencies

Chapter Learning Points:
• Challenges and skills of an experienced manager
• Begin the transition to leadership

The Management Map II **reference pages:** 1-15

Chapter Summary:
This chapter begins with a story of two managers: one who is beginning the management journey and one reflecting on what was learned on the road to becoming an experienced manager. You also are on the road to becoming an experienced manager. Since your first promotion to a managerial position you've gone through several business cycles, perfecting your skills in completing the various tasks and responsibilities required during each month of the year.

A list of skills and abilities of an experienced manager is supplied in this chapter to reflect on your competencies in each area. Just as new managers fall into typical traps, experienced managers have their own traps that are easy to tumble into, such as Lone Wolf, Missing in Action, Fear of Skill Obsolescence, or Interpersonally Unaware.

Finally, this chapter discusses the transition from manager to leader. It starts with having a vision for your team that relates to your organization's vision but is specifically targeted to the function you lead. True leaders can inspire their teams to greatness by communicating the vision and making it actionable by successful execution.

Your Initial Reflection:

What did you like best about the chapter? What topic resonated with you?

_____

_____

_____

Which concepts in the chapter apply to your department or organization?

_____

_____

_____

Which quote did you like from the chapter?

_____

_____

_____

Journey Progress — Check after you complete each activity:

❏ **Activity 1.1: Update Your Management Vision** — Reflect on how you envisioned the type of manager you would become and how that has changed with experience.

❏ **Activity 1.2: The Three C's of Management Review** — Describe how you have used the three C's of management: confidence, competence, and courage.

❏ **Activity 1.3: Experienced Manager Traps** — Identify typical experienced manager traps and develop plans to avoid them.

❏ **Activity 1.4: Experienced Manager Competencies** — Assess your competency in experienced manager skills.

❏ **Activity 1.5: Create a Vision for Your Team** — Create a vision for your team based on your company's vision.

❏ **Activity 1.6: Optional: Assess Your Leadership Style** — Complete a _Work of Leaders_ behavioral assessment and analyze the results.

Activity 1.1
Update Your Management Vision
The Management Map II reference pages 1-3

Activity Directions: In *TMM* participants completed a management vision statement based on how they saw their strengths as a manager, their values, and what they pictured people saying about them as managers at their retirement party. In this activity you will either copy your original vision or create an updated vision based on your management experience. **Individually complete the following questions:**

1. If you created a management vision when you were first promoted, record it here.

_____

_____

_____

2. Reflect on the type of manager you are now (your strengths as a manager), and what you learned about yourself since becoming a manager.

   Strengths: _____

   _____

   What I learned: _____

   _____

3. Finalize your management vision here. The vision statement should be descriptive of the type of manager you are now as well as what you strive to be. It is how you would like to be remembered as a manager. (See example below.)

   _____

   _____

   _____

Example: I am the type of manager who inspires and develops everyone on my team to be their best through training and coaching.

Activity Directions Continued: Share your vision with others and get feedback until you feel it is clear and a good reflection of what you want to be as a manager. Rewrite it on a sheet of paper or a card and put it where you can periodically reflect on your vision.

Activity 1.2

The Three C's of Management Review

The Management Map II **reference pages 3-4**

Activity Directions: Describe how you have used the three C's of management (competence, confidence, and courage) as an experienced manager. After you have individually answered how you have used each of the C's, gather a group of three to four of your peers to discuss how you would coach a new manager on developing each of the C's.

1. Develop confidence to perform your management role while being true to your vision.
   a) In what circumstances have you used confidence during your management journey to date?

   _____

   _____

   _____

   b) If you were coaching a new manager, how would you tell him/her to develop **confidence**?

   _____

   _____

   _____

2. Develop **competence** in using your skills and abilities to perform your role, while continuing to seek opportunities for continued improvement.
   a) In what circumstances have you used **competence** during your management journey to date?

   _____

   _____

   _____

   b) If you were coaching a new manager, how would you tell him/her to develop **competence**?

   _____

   _____

   _____

Activity 1.2 Continued

3. Develop **courage** to make the right decisions and not just the popular or easy decisions.

a) In what circumstances have you used **courage** during your management journey to date?

_____

_____

_____

b) If you were coaching a new manager, how would you tell him/her to develop **courage**?

_____

_____

_____

Activity 1.3
Experienced Manager Traps
The Management Map II reference pages 5-7

Activity Directions: As a new manager, you had to be cautious to not fall into the traps of Carrot and Stick, Apologetic, Buddy and Pal, and Do-It-Myself. Now it's time to identify if you fall into any of the experienced manager traps listed below.

1. Discuss the long-term consequences of each trap and then list steps on how to avoid one of the traps in question 2.

❑ **Lone Wolf** — Failure to seek out the opinions of others before making final decisions. Discuss the long-term consequences of being a Lone Wolf.

_____

❑ **Missing in Action** — Spending excessive time in meetings and working behind closed doors, resulting in not being available to the team members you lead. Discuss the long-term consequences of being Missing in Action.

_____

❑ **Fear of Skill Obsolescence** — When you realize that you are no longer the best "technical expert" in the group and you start taking on tasks that should be completed by your team members.
What are the long-term consequences of Fear of Skill Obsolescence?

_____

❑ **Interpersonally Unaware** — Demonstrating lack of empathy to others and not effectively reading the body language and voice tone to determine whether your message was effective.
What are the long-term consequences of being Interpersonally Unaware?

_____

2. Pick one of the traps, list ideas to avoid the trap, and develop an implementation plan:

_____

_____

_____

Activity 1.4
Experienced Manager Competencies
The Management Map II reference pages 7-8

Activity Directions: Assess your competency in each of the following experienced managerial skill areas using the rating key. The third column in the chart lists the chapter in *The Management Map II* where you can gain additional ideas on how to build the competency.

Rating key: 1 = proficient, 2 = acceptable, 3 = needs development

Rating	Competency		Chapter
	a)	Think strategically and participate in higher-level decision making	Two: Navigate Globally
	b)	Expand your perspective outside of your department into your company and industry	Two: Navigate Globally
	c)	Comprehend and manage the organizational culture of your department	Three: An Aerial View
	d)	Hire talented, highly engaged team members who fit within your culture	Four: All Aboard!
	e)	Create an environment where employees feel engaged and participatory	Five: All Hands on Deck
	f)	Challenge employees to grow in their abilities and careers by providing encouragement and direction	Seven: Create a Map for Others
	g)	Have the courage to confront challenging people-type situations and avoid the price of delay	Nine: Turbulence Ahead

1. Let's celebrate your strengths.

a) What is your best experienced manager competency?

_____

_____

b) Describe a specific example of how you have used this competency:

_____

_____

_____

Activity 1.4 Continued

2. Pick the competency you would like to develop during this course and also list the chapter number related to that competency. Take extra time in reading the identified chapter and completing the activities associated with that chapter.

   a) What experienced manager competency would you like to develop?

   _____

   _____

   b) List the chapter you would like to read in detail as well as other actions you can take to develop this competency:

   _____

   _____

   _____

   _____

   _____

   _____

   _____

Activity 1.5
Create a Vision for Your Team
The Management Map II reference pages 8-12

Activity Directions – Leaders focus on how their department contributes to the company's overall vision and creates an aligned vision for their team members. First list your organization's vision, and then create a vision for your team that will inspire commitment, focusing on connecting how each member's job contributes to the whole.

1. List your organization's vision. Take note of how it inspires you. (Example of an organizational vision for the San Diego Zoo: "To become a world leader at connecting people to wildlife and conservation.") (See page 10.)

   Your organization's vision:

   _____

   _____

   _____

2. What does your department do to contribute to your organization's vision? (Example: The marketing department at the San Diego Zoo would develop a website that encourages conservation.)

   How does your team of employees contribute to the vision of your organization?

   _____

   _____

   _____

3. Create an inspiring vision for your team of employees referencing the organization's vision and your department's function.

   _____

   _____

   _____

   _____

4. What will you do to create excitement around your vision and involve your team?

   _____

   _____

   _____

Practice communicating your vision and receive feedback from a peer.

Activity 1.6
Optional: Assess Your Leadership Style
The Management Map II reference page 14

Activity Directions – Take the leadership behavioral assessment *Work of Leaders* by Wiley Publishing. After you review your results, answer the questions below. Note that the closer your dot is the right on each continuum, the more you currently follow the leadership best practices.

1. What is your DiSC® style? _____
   Read page 4 in your *Work of Leaders* profile and make notes of valuable feedback.

   _____

   _____

   _____

2. What are the priorities that shape your leadership experience listed on page 5 in your *Work of Leaders* profile?

   _____

   _____

   _____

3. What are your greatest strengths? Located on page 20 of your *Work of Leaders* profile.

   _____

   _____

   _____

4. What are your greatest challenges? Located on pages 21-23 of your *Work of Leaders* profile. Complete "How Can You Adapt Your Behavior to Become a Better Leader."

   _____

   _____

   _____

TWO

NAVIGATE GLOBALLY
Understanding the External Marketplace

Items to Collect for This Chapter's Activities:
❑ A map of the USA or a world map, depending on where your organization is located and conducts business
❑ Diversity initiatives or statements by your company
❑ Picture of Saul Steinberg's 1976 *New Yorker* cover "View of the World from 9th Avenue"

Chapter Learning Points:
- Shift to a global viewpoint
- Think strategically

The Management Map II **reference pages:** 17-34

Chapter Summary:
Chapter two discusses the concept that the world seems to be getting smaller. Advances in transportation and technology make it possible for people from different nations, cultures, languages, and backgrounds to communicate, meet, and do business with one another. Globalization allows us to share ideas across the globe and it also is an opportunity for managers to increase their skills in managing a virtual team. There are different challenges when managing long-distance employees, including lack of "face time" with team members and more reliance on technology to effectively communicate.

Experienced managers know how to value diversity on their team, recognizing that everyone has something unique to contribute. They also regularly monitor their work area to ensure team members demonstrate cultural sensitively and inclusion with their coworkers.

The final section in this chapter introduces the concept of strategic thinking, sometimes referred to as "big picture thinking." Instead of just focusing on current internal factors, experienced managers scan external factors in the marketplace to predict the opportunities and threats that might be facing the company and industry in the future. Focusing on strategic thinking will enlarge a manager's field of vision, which will put them in a place to recommend breakthrough ideas to create a competitive advantage now and in the future.

Your Initial Reflection:
What did you like best about the chapter? What topic resonated with you?

_____

_____

_____

Which concepts in the chapter apply to your department or organization?

_____

_____

_____

Which quote did you like from the chapter?

_____

_____

_____

Journey Progress — Check after you complete each activity:

☐ **Activity 2.1: Describe Your Organization** — Understand your company's industry, products and services, customers, and marketplace.

☐ **Activity 2.2: Communicate Virtually** — Collect technology resources for communicating long distance with team members, customers, and vendors.

☐ **Activity 2.3: Cultural Diversity and Sensitivity** — Analyze the importance of valuing diversity and organizational policies on diversity.

☐ **Activity 2.4: Cultural Survey** — Read and reflect on questions to analyze cultural sensitivity in your department.

☐ **Activity 2.5: Environmental Scan** – Use the acronym PESTEL to reflect on the external forces impacting your organization and industry.

☐ **Activity 2.6: SWOT Analysis** – Analyze internal strengths and weaknesses and external opportunities and threats.

Activity 2.1
Describe Your Organization
The Management Map II reference pages 17-20

Activity Directions: In this activity you will gather key information about your organization. Understanding what makes your organization unique will aid in developing your strategic decision making. Complete the questions individually or with a group of your peer managers.

1. List the products and services provided by your organization.

_____

_____

_____

2. Based on the list of products and services you made in question 1, list your organization's industries. The Bureau of Labor Statistics (BLS) website bls.gov/iag/tgs/iag_index_naics.htm has list of "Industries at a Glance" that can assist you with this question.

_____

_____

_____

Activity Directions continued: Obtain either a map of the USA or a world map, depending on where your organization is located and conducts business.

3. Place a dot on the locations of your corporate headquarters and other offices/plants on your map. List locations here:

_____

_____

_____

Activity 2.1 Continued

4. Describe the marketplace for your organization. Place a dot (different color than the dot used in question 3 on the locations of your customers.

_____

_____

_____

5. List several of your key competitors below. Place a dot (use a third color) on the locations of your competitors.

_____

_____

_____

6. **Post Work Activity:** Share your map with the employees on your team; consider posting it in your work area.

Activity 2.2
Communicate Virtually
The Management Map II **reference pages 20-22**

Activity Directions: It has become increasingly common to have virtual team members. Virtual team members are those who are not located in the same building as their manager. Long distances between the manager and team members present unique communication challenges. List all the methods of technology and communication methods available to you and how you utilize them. If you are not sure what is available, make an appointment with your IT department to learn more. If you belong to a professional networking group, ask which methods other organizations use to communicate over long distances.

Method	How I will use this method
Example: Facetime	The application Facetime can be used for one-on-one discussions with virtual employees.

Activity 2.3
Cultural Diversity and Sensitivity
The Management Map II reference pages 22-26

Activity Directions: Best practices were not all born in just one civilization. The world that we live in today is a result of many cultures coming together. Answer the following reflective questions regarding cultural diversity either individually or with a group of peer managers.

1. List three reasons why cultural diversity and cultural sensitivity are important for your department and organization:

   a) _____

   b) _____

   c) _____

2. Does your organization have a diversity policy or cultural sensitivity statement? If yes, list the key elements of the statement here:

   _____

   _____

   _____

3. Conduct an internet search for a sample cultural diversity policy statement from another organization. List the key elements from the statement:

   _____

   _____

   _____

4. Compare your organization's policy with the statement you located. What do they have in common and how are they different?

   _____

   _____

   _____

Activity 2.4
Cultural Survey
The Management Map II reference pages 24-26

Activity Directions: Experienced managers have a well-developed sense of cultural sensitivity. These managers regularly monitor their work area to ensure everyone on the team feels respected and has the opportunity to make a contribution. Think about your work group as you read each of the following cultural sensitivity situations. Check the column for how often this occurs in your area.

Situation	Regularly Occurs	Sometimes Occurs	Never Occurs
1. Some of your team members create "cliques" where others are excluded.			
2. Only a few members of your team feel free to contribute new ideas; many are not participative.			
3. Some team members appear to be isolated from the group.			
4. Dietary restrictions and preferences are not considered when ordering team lunches or other snacks.			
5. Employees feel pressured to participate in holiday and birthday celebrations.			
6. Recognition is not customized to fit the desires of each team member. For example, some team members are uncomfortable with public recognition.			
7. Words, phrases, and/or jokes have entered into the vocabulary of your department that might be offensive to others.			

Choose one of the situations that you rated either Regularly or Sometimes Occurs and list it here along with an action plan to correct the situation:

Situation number: _____

Action Plan: _____

_____

_____

_____

Activity 2.5
Environmental Scan
The Management Map II reference pages 27-29

Activity Directions: Complete an environmental scan for your organization. Read each definition in *TMM II* on pages 27-29 as you complete the factors in PESTEL: Political, Economic, Social, Technological, Environmental, and Legal. Either complete this activity individually or gather a group of your peer managers in order to share ideas.

1. Political factors that impact my organization/industry:

_____

_____

_____

2. Economic factors that impact my organization/industry:

_____

_____

_____

3. Social factors that impact my organization/industry:

_____

_____

_____

4. Technological factors that impact my organization/industry:

_____

_____

_____

5. Environmental factors that impact my organization/industry:

_____

_____

_____

Activity 2.5 Continued

6. Legal factors that impact my organization/industry:

_____

_____

_____

Share your notes with your manager, ask for his/her perspective, and add the input to your notes in each area.

Activity 2.6
SWOT Analysis
The Management Map II reference pages 30-32

Activity Directions: After you complete an environmental scan using PESTEL, it is important to synthesize the items listed as opportunities and strengths in a SWOT analysis. Then, add an analysis of your organization's internal strengths and weaknesses to complete the SWOT. The questions in each box can be used as a guideline for your answers.

Strengths – Sample questions: What are our advantages? What do other people see as our strengths? What is something that our customers value that our competition doesn't have or do? **Notes:**	**Weaknesses** – Sample questions: What could we improve? What does our competition do better? What complaints do we get from our customers? **Notes:**
Opportunities – Sample questions: What are the external trends that are related to our business? What does the market need that we could provide? How are we positioned to take advantage of current and future trends? **Notes:**	**Threats** – Sample questions: What obstacles do we face? What new trends could make us obsolete? Is our competition better equipped to meet future changes in the marketplace? **Notes:**

THREE

AN AERIAL VIEW
Examining Your Corporate Culture

Items to Collect for This Chapter's Activities:
❑ Descriptions of your organization's culture
❑ Samples of other organization's culture descriptions

Chapter Learning Points:
- Identify your organization's corporate culture
- Become a caretaker of culture

The Management Map II **reference pages:** 35-46

Chapter Summary:
The chapter begins with a definition of culture shock, which is the feeling of disorientation experienced by someone who is suddenly subjected to an unfamiliar culture. Culture shock can also be experienced in a work environment when you accept a position in a new company.

It may be very difficult to describe your company's culture because of how immersed we become after working in one company for a long period of time. The longer the organization is in existence, the more highly developed its culture will be. Culture can be described by examining the following areas: decision making, rewards/recognition, coaching/discipline, and communication.

The chapter concludes with the importance for experienced managers to create culture congruency. To be congruent is when your stated culture is compatible with the actual policies, process, and procedures in place. Congruency impacts credibility and competence. Six situations were presented in this chapter to examine congruency issues and the possible consequence if incompatible.

Your Initial Reflection:
What did you like best about the chapter? What topic resonated with you?

_____

_____

_____

Which concepts in the chapter apply to your department or organization?

_____

_____

_____

Which quote did you like from the chapter?

_____

_____

_____

Journey Progress — Check after you complete each activity:

☐ **Activity 3.1: Culture Shock Experience** — Respond to reflection questions on your experiences with culture shock.

☐ **Activity 3.2: Analyze Your Corporate Culture** — Analyze and discuss different characteristics that describe your organization's culture.

☐ **Activity 3.3: Supporting Your Culture** — Based on the analysis of your organization's culture characteristics in Activity 3.2, list actions you can take to support your culture.

☐ **Activity 3.4: Explore Culture Congruency** — Analyze situations to determine if there is congruency with the culture of the organization as well as the impact of the incongruences.

Activity 3.1
Culture Shock Experience
The Management Map II reference pages 35-37

Activity Directions: Culture shock is the feeling of disorientation experienced by someone who is suddenly subjected to an unfamiliar culture or way of life. Experienced managers have empathy for new employees who may have culture shock when they join their organization. A good way to develop empathy is to reflect on your own experiences as you answer the following questions. Discuss your answers with a peer manager.

1. Think about a time when you've traveled to another country or even a different area of your own county. What surprised you about their culture compared to yours? What did you miss about your own culture?

_____

_____

_____

_____

2. Compare two companies you've worked for in the past. How did their cultures differ? What did you expect when you went to work for each company and how did the experience differ from your expectations?

_____

_____

_____

_____

3. Has a new employee ever complained, "You do so many things differently here compared to my last company." How could this culture shock have been avoided?

_____

_____

_____

_____

Activity 3.2
Analyze Your Corporate Culture
The Management Map II reference pages 37-40

Activity Directions: Reread the definition of the different culture characteristics on pages 39-40 and evaluate your organization in each characteristic by placing a dot along each line. After individually completing the chart, compare your answers with others in your organization.

Characteristic	Place a Dot on Each Line
Decision Making	Fast _____ Slow
Formality	Formal _____ Informal
Teamwork	Collaboration _____ Individualism
Innovation	High Risk Taking _____ Risk Averse
Conflict Tolerance	Encouraged _____ Avoided

1. When you compared your dot placement with others in the organization, did they agree or disagree with your answers? Which characteristics were rated differently?

_____

_____

_____

2. Discuss what is great about your culture and what aspects of your culture that might be might be barriers to success.

Great About Our Culture	Barriers in Our Culture

Activity 3.3
Supporting Your Culture
The Management Map II reference pages 40-42

Activity Directions: Managers are a key ingredient in creating and maintaining corporate culture. How are you reinforcing your corporate culture during your everyday managerial responsibilities? Refer to your answers in Activity 3.2 as you complete this chart. List specific actions you will take to support your organization's culture for each activity. Pick any characteristic that fits the activity; there is room for you to list two but feel free to only choose one. An example is provided for Orientation.

Activities	**Characteristic	Action Plans
Example: Orientation	**Teamwork –** Collaborative	Make orientation for new employees collaborative by involving all members of our team.
	Formality – Formal	Create a checklist of topics and assigned responsibilities for new hire orientation.
Staffing		
Rewards/Recognition		
Coaching/Discipline		
Communication		

Characteristics:
- **Decision making** – Fast/slow
- **Formality** – Formal/informal
- **Teamwork** – Collaboration/individualism
- **Innovation** – High risk taking/risk averse
- **Conflict tolerance** – Encouraged/avoided

Activity 3.4

Explore Culture Congruency

The Management Map II reference pages 42-44

Activity Directions: Change initiatives will fail or cause major disruption in the workplace if they are incongruent with the corporate culture. Either individually or with a group of peer managers, read the following situations and list the congruency issues and consequences. An example is provided for situation 1.

Situation	Issues and Consequences
1. Your values statement includes creativity and innovation in a culture with low tolerance for risk. It takes three review committees and six levels of signatures to approve a new product. What is the result?	Situation Issues: • The values statement and what actually occurs in the organization do not appear congruent.
	Situation Consequences: • Employees will not take the values statement seriously. • Newly hired employees who value creativity and innovation will feel stifled by bureaucracy.
2. You are introducing a productivity-based bonus plan in a culture that values quality over quantity. Specific volume requirements will be established for each position.	Situation Issues: Situation Consequences:
3. Your organization has a formal, hierarchal culture. You want to focus on employee involvement by encouraging self-directed work teams to make decisions and question the status quo. If the concept is successful, a layer of management may be removed.	Situation Issues: Situation Consequences:

Activity 3.4 Continued

Situation	Issues and Consequences
4. You have a culture that is team oriented and parental. You have always paid all benefits in full for employees and given profit sharing to everyone. Due to cost increases, you would like employees to start paying for part of their benefit cost. You also want to make the profit sharing based on individual performance.	Situation Issues: Situation Consequences:
5. Your company value statement says the company rewards and recognizes individuality, but your performance reviews and rewards are based on team results.	Situation Issues: Situation Consequences:
6. Your company establishes a goal for a certain amount of training hours employees are expected to attend each year. In reality, the pressure to achieve results and the pace of the workplace doesn't allow time off for training.	Situation Issues: Situation Consequences:

FOUR

ALL ABOARD!
Acquiring Talent

Items to Collect for This Chapter's Activities:
- ❑ Process for requisitioning a new employee
- ❑ Job descriptions for frequently open jobs in your area
- ❑ Company specific instructions on interviewing, selection, and onboarding

Chapter Learning Points:
- Recognize characteristics of top talent
- Create onboarding for new team members

The Management Map II **reference pages:** 47-68

Chapter Summary:
The chapter begins with discussing the important managerial role of acquiring talent. Experienced managers also understand that it is critical to hire the right people with the best skills and abilities that fit the culture of their organization. When the mentality switches from "hiring warm bodies" to "hire the best," it can have a significant positive impact on the organization.

A five-step process for hiring the best people was outlined: 1) Forecast staffing needs, 2) Identify critical success factors, 3) Develop interview questions, 4) Interview candidates, and 5) Provide a realistic job preview. Details are provided for each step in the process. The hiring process described should be reviewed with your human resource department to ensure it complies with your organization's policy and procedures.

Finally, the chapter concludes with discussing a method for onboarding new employees in order to build their commitment and engagement with their new manager, team members, and their organization.

Your Initial Reflection:
What did you like best about the chapter? What topic resonated with you?

_____

_____

_____

Which concepts in the chapter apply to your department or organization?

_____

_____

_____

Which quote did you like from the chapter?

_____

_____

_____

Journey Progress — Check after you complete each activity:

☐ **Activity 4.1: Forecast Your Staffing Needs** — Respond to questions to determine your staffing needs for next year.

☐ **Activity 4.2: Identify Critical Success Factors** — Locate a job description and identify the critical success factors for the position.

☐ **Activity 4.3: Develop Interview Questions** — Select several of the critical success factors identified in the last activity and create behavior based interview questions.

☐ **Activity 4.4: Create a Realistic Job Preview** — Use the show-tell-do approach in planning a realistic job preview.

☐ **Activity 4.5: Obtain Input about Onboarding** — Meet with a recently hired team member to discuss his or her onboarding experience.

☐ **Activity 4.6: Plan Changes to Your Onboarding Process** — Create a plan to improve your onboarding process based on input received in Activity 4.5.

Activity 4.1
Forecast Your Staffing Needs
The Management Map II **reference pages 50-52**

Activity Directions: There are several decisions to consider around when and if you should replace employees who leave your organization. But why wait until someone leaves to forecast your staffing needs? By examining staffing patterns you can create an effective staffing needs forecast and be better prepared for the future. Complete the following analysis to forecast your staffing needs for next year:

1. Total number of employees in your department: _____

2. The number of employees who left your department last year:

Resigned:	
Transferred:	
Terminated:	
Total:	

3. Based on the workload changes you expect in the coming year (i.e., number of clients, changes in efficiency, etc.), project your staffing needs here:

   Workload will (check one):   ____Increase   ____Decrease   ____Stay Even

4. Enter the estimated number of people you will hire next year by position title:

Number	Position Title

5. When you replace exiting employees, are there skills you would like to add in your department? List skills here:

_____

_____

_____

Activity 4.2
Identify Critical Success Factors
The Management Map II reference pages 53-55

Activity Directions: Critical success factors include those skills, abilities, and previous experience that will turn a candidate into a successful, productive team member. Success factors can also relate to education, training, and technical ability as well as interpersonal skills, culture fit, values match, and ability to work required hours. Locate a job description for a position in your team and answer the following questions. See the Receptionist's example on pages 53-54.

1. Job Title: _____

2. Review the responsibility or job duties section of the job description. Circle items that are critical success factors and list a few here:

    _____

    _____

    _____

3. Review the requirements section of the job description such as knowledge, skills, education, and experience. Circle items that are critical success factors and list a few here:

    _____

    _____

    _____

4. Review the aspects of your cultural analysis from Activity 3.2 that would identify critical success factors and list a few here:

    _____

    _____

    _____

Show your analysis to your manager or a member of human resources for feedback.

Activity 4.3

Develop Interview Questions

The Management Map II reference pages 55-59

Activity Directions: Refer to the critical success factors you identified in Activity 4.2. Copy several of the factors to the first column on the chart. Then write a behavioral-based question designed to encourage a response on how the candidate has used the skill or ability in the past. An example for the receptionist position is provided at the bottom of the page.

Critical Success Factor	Interview Question

Receptionist Example:

Critical Success Factor	Interview Question
Multiple Priorities	Tell me about a day when you dealt with multiple priorities. What did you do to prioritize and what was the result?
Interpersonal Skills	Give me a specific example of when you had to use your interpersonal skills with a caller who was confused or angry.
Industry Experience	Describe the different industries where you've held positions in the past. How does your experience compare with our industry?
Interacting with Public	Face-to-face customer interaction is slightly different than over-the-phone communication. Tell me about a situation in the past where you successfully interacted with a customer in person.

Activity 4.4
Create a Realistic Job Preview
The Management Map II reference pages 59-61

Activity Directions: A realistic job preview (RJP) provides candidates with an inside look at duties and environment of the position within your organization. The most effective RJP immerses the candidate in the work environment to avoid "buyer's remorse." Think about the show-tell-try approach on pages 60-61 as you respond to the following questions:

1. What are the things you can **show** candidates about your organization and open position?

_____

_____

_____

_____

2. What are topics you can **tell** candidates about your organization and open position?

_____

_____

_____

3. Is it possible for the candidate to actually **try** a piece of the job? Make a list of the tasks the candidate can try on the job. Check with your human resources department to make sure your **try** idea doesn't violate policies or laws.

_____

_____

_____

Activity 4.5
Obtain Input about Onboarding
The Management Map II **reference pages 62-66**

Activity Directions: I'm sure you've heard the quote "You'll never have a second chance to create a first impression." This is especially true when onboarding new team members. Who better to ask than someone who has recently experienced your onboarding process? Interview a recently hired team member to gain onboarding ideas from his or her perspective.

1. What was effective about the onboarding you received when you joined our organization?

_____

_____

_____

2. Was the onboarding process the same or different than your expectations?

_____

_____

_____

3. What actions would have made you feel more welcome on your first day, and during your first week?

First Day	First Week

4. What other ideas do you have to improve our onboarding process?

_____

_____

Activity 4.6

Plan Changes to Your Onboarding Process
The Management Map II reference pages 62-66

Activity Directions: This activity is a continuation of Activity 4.5. Reflect on the information you received from the employee interview as well as other ideas you have. List your plan below. An example is provided on the first line. Be sure to review your plan with your manager or a member of human resources, obtaining approval for any cost increases to the process.

Onboarding Action Ideas	Timetable
Example: *Create a "first day buddy" program*	Next week

FIVE

ALL HANDS ON DECK...
Building a Strong Team

Items to Collect for This Chapter's Activities:
❑ Information on the type of team-building activities your organization supports
❑ A picture of how an orchestra is arranged

Chapter Learning Points:
• Understand characteristics of effective teams
• Build a team environment

***The Management Map II* reference pages:** 69-88

Chapter Summary:
The chapter begins with an analogy of how a manager is like an orchestra conductor. Both start out their career with a specialty, but then when it comes time to lead others they expand past their own area of expertise to understand how every skill and function fits into the "big picture."

Teamwork is the process of working collaboratively with a group of people to achieve a goal. The challenge is to first create teamwork among the group you manage and then draw the connection of how their work contributes to their customers. When you value the different strengths of a diverse workforce you can create innovative products and services. The power of teamwork can be harnessed when implementing change in your organization.

The chapter concludes with identifying ineffective teamwork and tips to improve teamwork. To improve teamwork, many organizations have team-building sessions. To be truly effective, team-building sessions should contain three phases: action, reflection, and implementation. Team sharing is another popular method of improving teamwork and several examples were provided.

Your Initial Reflection:
What did you like best about the chapter? What topic resonated with you?

_____

_____

_____

Which concepts in the chapter apply to your department or organization?

_____

_____

_____

Which quote did you like from the chapter?

_____

_____

_____

Journey Progress — Check after you complete each activity:

☐ **Activity 5.1: Your Experience with Teams** — Make a list of characteristics of effective and ineffective teams.

☐ **Activity 5.2: Analyze Your Team** — Compare two lists of team characteristics by reflecting on the current team you lead.

☐ **Activity 5.3: The Strengths of Your Team** — Draw a layout of your team based on their strengths, similar to an orchestra layout.

☐ **Activity 5.4: Team Ground Rules** — Hold a brainstorming session with your team to create team ground rules.

☐ **Activity 5.5: Team-building Activity** — Hold a team-building activity with your team.

Activity 5.1

Your Experience with Teams
The Management Map II reference pages 76-81

Activity Directions: I'm sure that you've been part of many teams in your life. Think about effective and ineffective teams of which you've been a member and identify the characteristics of both in the chart below. After completing the charts, place a star next to the top three characteristics on the "effective" side that you want to make sure you capture for the team you lead now.

Ineffective Team Characteristics	Effective Team Characteristics

Activity 5.2

Analyze Your Team

The Management Map II reference pages 79-81

Activity Directions: Consider the two teams described below. Place checkmarks next to the sentences that describe the team you lead now. After completing the activity, answer the question that follows the chart.

Team A Characteristics	Team B Characteristics
❏ Tap into the skills and opinions of all team members	❏ Are unwilling to brainstorm, compromise, share ideas, and support one another
❏ End discussions with clear and specific resolutions and calls to action	❏ Waste time on politics, personal attacks, and destructive conflict
❏ Make better, faster decisions	❏ Revisit past discussions and decisions again and again
❏ Achieve buy-in from everyone and focus on the right issues	❏ Avoid face-to-face discussions and vent in the hallway
❏ Are personally invested, accountable, and engaged in achieving results	❏ Miss deadlines and key deliverables
❏ Aren't afraid to speak up when they think the team is going in the wrong direction	❏ Blame others when mistakes are made instead of reaching out to provide assistance
❏ Trust the team to discuss their strengths and weaknesses and are able to ask for help when needed	❏ Are passive aggressive by agreeing to a course of action in meetings but then taking different actions back on the job

You may have noticed that Team A describes effective team characteristics. Did you check any items in the Team B column? If yes, pick one of the bullet points you checked and create an action plan to improve in that area.

_____

_____

_____

_____

_____

_____

Activity 5.3

The Strengths of Your Team
The Management Map II reference pages 71-74

Activity Directions: Picture a layout of an orchestra or perform an internet search to locate a sample layout. There are sections of an orchestra, and just like your team members, each have talents. Just as an orchestra leader brings different sections of the orchestra into the musical piece at the right time, a manager can utilize the right team member talent at the right time. For example, do you need creativity to bring new ideas to a team project? "Point your baton" to the creative group in your orchestra. Group your team members in the space below in a similar way an orchestra is organized. Note that some of your team members may fall into more than one talent category.

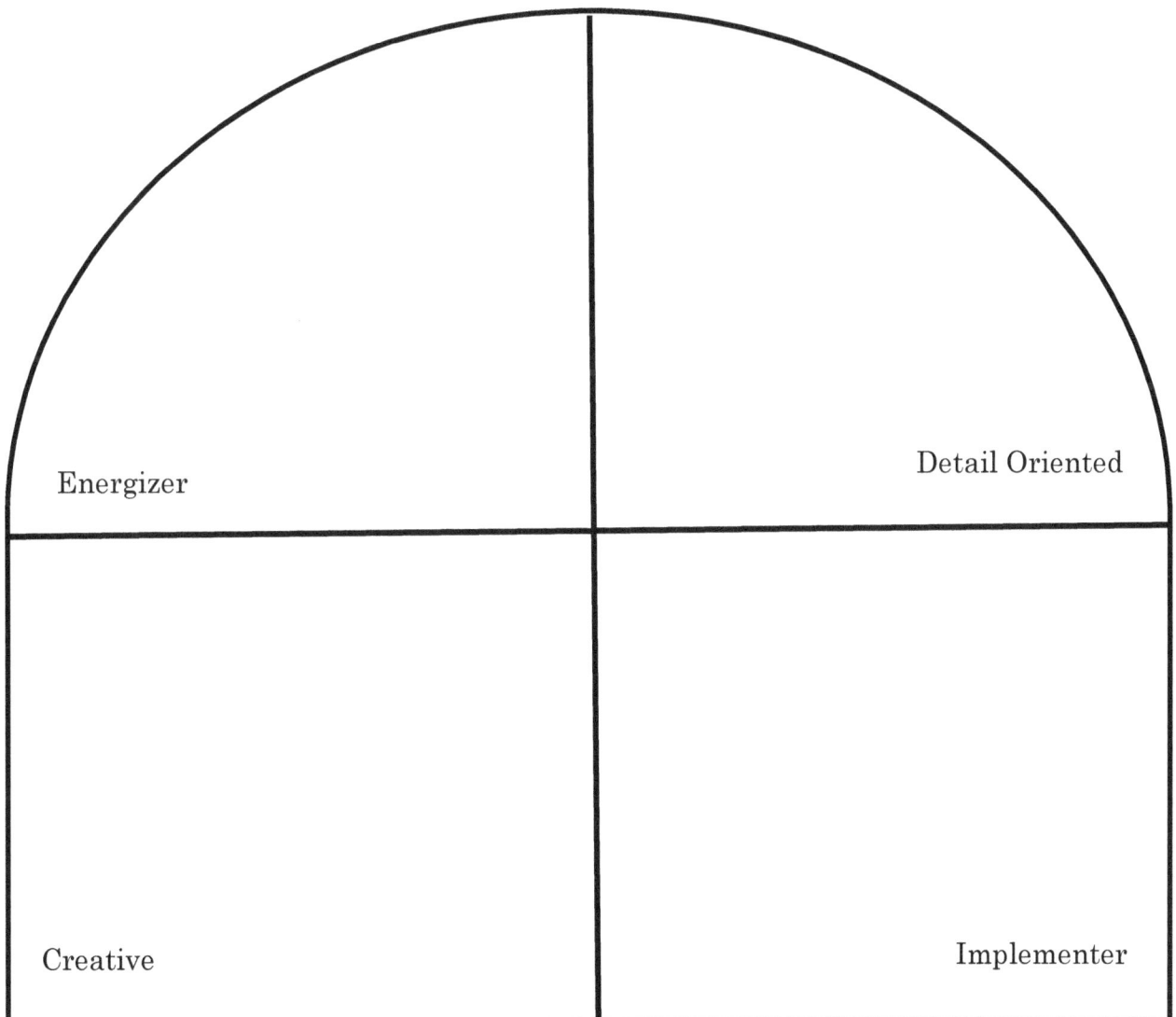

Energizer

Detail Oriented

Creative

Implementer

Activity 5.4

Team Ground Rules

The Management Map II reference pages 82-83

Activity Directions: Team ground rules are guidelines for how team members interact with each other and contribute to team meetings and other interactions. One of the benefits of ground rules is that they establish specific expectations as defined by the team members themselves. Lead a brainstorming session with your team to create ground rules. Use flip chart paper or a white board to capture everyone's ideas in full view of the whole team. Provide team members with examples before the meeting so they can be thinking about the best ground rules for their team.

Examples of team ground rules:
- Begin and end all meetings on time.
- Develop positive relationships with all team members.
- Participate to the fullest of your ability.
- Encourage everyone to participate.
- Offer solutions, not just problems.
- Make every effort to meet commitments

Record final ground rules here:
_____
_____
_____
_____
_____
_____
_____
_____
_____
_____
_____

Type ground rules and display at all team meetings and/or work area and also provide them to new employees who join your team.

Activity 5.5
Team-building Activity
The Management Map II reference pages 81-86

Activity Directions: Successful teamwork is built on a foundation of trust. Trust is improved by understanding each team member better. Lead a team-building session with your team of employees. Use one of the activities mentioned on pages 82-85 or locate another team-building activity that fits the action-reflection-implementation model described on pages 81-82. Debrief your experience by answering the questions below:

1. Which team-building activity did you use? Describe it here.

_____

_____

_____

2. What was the reaction of your team as they went through the activity?

_____

_____

_____

3. What feedback did you hear from your team members after the activity? Were your employees able to implement ideas back on the job or did the activity improve the way they worked together?

_____

_____

_____

SIX

COMMITMENT TO THE JOURNEY
Building Engagement at Work

Items to Collect for This Chapter's Activities:
❑ Results and information around your organization's climate or engagement surveys
❑ Turnover statistics in your department over the last year

Chapter Learning Points:
- Define employee engagement
- Create an environment that engages others

The Management Map II **reference pages:** 89-108

Chapter Summary:
The chapter begins with a definition of employee engagement as "a person who is fully involved in and enthusiastic about his or her work." Three employee engagement levels are identified: engaged, not engaged, and actively disengaged. A short story at the beginning of the chapter demonstrated behavior in each area.

There are barriers that prevent employees from being engaged at work. Those barriers include Unfulfilled Expectations, Organizational Changes, and Personal Circumstances. If experienced managers understand why each of the three barriers are a problem and their role in the removal or reduction of the barriers, they can directly impact employee engagement. A case study demonstrating how a manager uses techniques to remove barriers is included in this chapter as well as a way to measure engagement.

The chapter concludes with the retention question "How do you know that someone is thinking about leaving your organization?" Six tips for improving employee retention in your organization are presented: 1) Identify early warning signs, 2) Recognize and celebrate success, 3) Get to know your employees as individuals, 4) Discuss advancement and development, 5) Create line of sight to outcomes, and 6) Assess engagement.

Your Initial Reflection:
What did you like best about the chapter? What topic resonated with you?

_____

_____

_____

Which concepts in the chapter apply to your department or organization?

_____

_____

_____

Which quote did you like from the chapter?

_____

_____

_____

Journey Progress — Check after you complete each activity:

☐ **Activity 6.1: Engagement Behaviors** — Develop a list of behaviors in each engagement category.

☐ **Activity 6.2: Current Workforce Engagement** — Determine the percentage of your current team who are engaged, not engaged, and actively disengaged.

☐ **Activity 6.3: Engagement Discussion** — Hold a discussion with one of your engaged team members and a team member who is not engaged.

☐ **Activity 6.4: Engagement Barrier: Organizational Change** — Analyze an organizational change that might impact the engagement of your team.

☐ **Activity 6.5: Employee Retention** — Identify early warning signs that may lead to employee turnover.

Activity 6.1

Engagement Behaviors

The Management Map II reference pages 89-91

Activity Directions: Curt Coffman, co-author of the book *First Break All the Rules* identifies three types of engagement: engaged employees, not engaged employees, and actively disengaged employees. Reread the definitions of the three engagement categories on page 90 and describe the behaviors in each category.

1. Describe behaviors that can be observed in **engaged employees** (i.e., what they are likely to do and say):

_____

_____

_____

_____

2. Describe behaviors that can be observed in **not engaged employees** (i.e., what they are likely to do and say):

_____

_____

_____

_____

3. Describe behaviors that can be observed in **actively disengaged employees** (i.e., what they are likely to do and say):

_____

_____

_____

_____

Activity 6.2
Current Workforce Engagement
The Management Map II reference pages 90-92

Activity Directions: Based on the behaviors you described in Activity 6.1, indicate your best estimate of the percentage of your team that falls into each engagement category and the impact on the work climate in your department.

Category	Percent of Workforce
Engaged employees	
Not engaged employees	
Actively disengaged employees	

1. List one thing you can keep doing to keep your **engaged employees** fully engaged:

   _____

   _____

   _____

2. List one thing you can do to move **not engaged employees** to the **engaged employees** category:

   _____

   _____

   _____

3. List one thing you can do to improve the engagement of **actively disengaged employees**:

   _____

   _____

   _____

Activity 6.3
Engagement Discussion
The Management Map II **reference pages 90-99**

Activity Directions: Identify someone in your department who exhibits full engagement and another one who appears not to be engaged. Hold a discussion with each employee, encouraging open dialog. The purpose of the discussions are to make sure your engaged employee stays engaged and your not-engaged employee becomes more engaged; take notes on any action plans created. Suggested discussion flow appears below:

Discussion outline:
1. Show sincere appreciation for the personal contribution the person makes to the department. Be as specific as possible with your examples.
2. Define engagement at work to your employee (read description on page 90).
3. Ask your employee to identify situations that create barriers to their feeling engaged at work.
4. Discuss how to remove or reduce barriers.

Discussion summary and action plans from your **engaged employee** discussion:

_____

_____

_____

_____

_____

Discussion summary and action plans from your **not engaged employee** discussion:

_____

_____

_____

_____

_____

Activity 6.4

Engagement Barrier: Organizational Change

The Management Map II **reference pages 93-99**

Activity Directions: Engagement barriers are those things that prevent someone from being engaged at work. Leaders have the ability to become change agents who understand how change impacts engagement and create plans for smooth and successful transitions. Organizational changes in the following areas are likely to cause reduced engagement:

Organizational Changes:
1. Job expectations have changed
2. New rules or procedures were introduced
3. Shortage of resources has occurred
4. Workload has increased or decreased
5. Work hours have changed
6. A new manager or team members have been added to the group

Directions continued: Choose one of the changes above that are about to occur in your organization, or list another change experience, and respond to the following questions: (see example on page 93)

The change situation:

_____

_____

_____

1. Why is the change necessary and what is driving the change?

_____

_____

_____

2. How does the change negatively impact my team members? Would some team members be impacted more than others?

_____

_____

_____

Activity 6.4 Continued

3. How does the change positively impact my team members? What are the positive impact items I can share with my team?

_____

_____

_____

4. In what ways can I assist my team members in adapting to this change?

_____

_____

_____

5. What barriers exist in our successfully adapting to this change?

_____

_____

_____

6. How can I enlist my team members' help in removing the restraining forces of change through involvement and problem solving?

_____

_____

_____

_____

Activity 6.5
Employee Retention
The Management Map II reference pages 101-105

Activity Directions: Early warning signs are changes in behavior that may indicate a key player is looking outside the company for a new job. First, indicate your turnover compared to the previous year in the box below. Then think back on the behavior of the employees who left, and place a check mark next to all the early warning signs you noticed.

The number of people who have left your team in the last twelve months: _____
The number of people who left your team who were key players: _____

✔	Early Warning Signs
	The person's work productivity had decreased more than usual.
	The person acted less like a team player than usual.
	The person had been less willing to commit to long-term timelines than usual.
	The person exhibited less effort and work motivation than usual.
	The person left work early or arrived late more frequently than usual.
	The person showed less interest in working with customers than usual.
	The person had been more withdrawn and less participative than usual.
	The person complained about minor things about the company more than usual.

Questions for Discussion:

1. Which of the early warnings signs were observed most often before employees left?

_____

_____

2. What will you do differently the next time you observe early warning signs, especially in key players on your team?

_____

_____

SEVEN

CREATE A MAP FOR OTHERS...
Career Planning for Your Team

Items to Collect for This Chapter's Activities:
☐ Career resources offered at your company
☐ Job description for a supervisory position

Chapter Learning Points:

- Hold career planning discussions
- Understand steps for succession planning

The Management Map II **reference pages:** 109-124

Chapter Summary:
The chapter begins with a comparison of how career planning is like navigating a shopping mall with store directories. Everyone has different interests in places to shop just like everyone has different career interests. To get to your destination in both planning a shopping route or a career, it is equally important to know the "you are here" as well as "where you want to go." Managers can act like a store directory by probing employees for their career interests, showing employees the career path to get there, and the "you are here" based on their current skills and experience.

There is a new definition of career success and five different employee circumstances were presented to provide examples of how conversations may differ based on the employee's goals and their current "you are here." There is also a new definition of development. It no longer just means "send them to a training class." Development has more to do with your employee's goals and how that person likes to learn.

The chapter ends with a discussion of the importance of succession planning, with an example of how the process contributes to career planning.

Your Initial Reflection:

What did you like best about the chapter? What topic resonated with you?

_____

_____

_____

Which concepts in the chapter apply to your department or organization?

_____

_____

_____

Which quote did you like from the chapter?

_____

_____

_____

Journey Progress — Check after you complete each activity:

❒ **Activity 7.1: Concerns about Career Discussions** — List your concerns around holding career discussions.

❒ **Activity 7.2: Career Planning Resources** — Locate resources available for career planning at your organization.

❒ **Activity 7.3: Career Mapping** — Create a diagram with a "you are here" for an employee and what he or she would need to do to prepare for a future destination.

❒ **Activity 7.4: Hold Career Discussions** — Hold career conversations with at least two employees on your team.

❒ **Activity 7.5: Brainstorm Skill Development** — Brainstorm methods for developing skills in several areas.

Activity 7.1
Concerns about Career Discussions
The Management Map II **reference pages 111-114**

Activity Directions: Employees typically want opportunities to discuss their career advancement and expect their manager to initiate discussions. Managers, however, normally have concerns about holding career discussions. Rate the fears around career discussions listed below and pick out your biggest concern. Work with a partner to discuss how to overcome this fear.

Rating Scale: 1: High Concern, **2:** Mild Concern, **3:** No Concern

Rating	Concern
	1. Fear of telling the employee there aren't any openings right now for promotion.
	2. Fear of losing your most productive employee to another department.
	3. Fear of not having the budget to offer employees training and development opportunities.
	4. Fear if you bring up career planning with your employee you might be setting expectations that can't be delivered.
	5. Fear that if you discuss careers with employees who don't want a promotion, you might be causing them discomfort.
	6. Fear that employees will have lofty career goals that don't match their skills and abilities, which can lead to having to tell the employee they aren't qualified.
	7. Fear that employees will expect you as their manager to assume total responsibility for their career and training.

Brainstorm how to overcome your number one concern about career discussions:

_____

_____

_____

_____

Activity 7.2
Career Planning Resources
The Management Map II reference pages 114-119

Activity Directions: Your organization may offer resources to assist you in holding career discussions with employees. Listed below are typical career resources offered by organizations. Check all that apply to your company:

✔	Career Discussion Resource
	Job descriptions
	Job postings
	Cross-training opportunities
	Mentor programs
	Tuition reimbursement
	Career maps or ladders
	Learning management system (LMS) to schedule or deliver training
	Book clubs on professional development
	Succession planning

Questions for Discussion:

1. Which resources do you regularly utilize at your organization?

_____

_____

2. Which of the career resources listed will you begin to use more frequently?

_____

_____

_____

Activity 7.3
Career Mapping
The Management Map II reference pages 112-117

Activity Directions: In this activity you will identify a current employee's position on your team in the top box. In the bottom box, describe a possible future position. For example, a supervisor position. In the center box, list all the skills and experience the employee would need to prepare for this future position.

Describe employee's current position (the "you are here"):

List the skills, education, and experience needed before moving to the future destination:

Describe a future new role (the "destination"):

Activity 7.4
Hold Career Discussions
The Management Map II reference pages 109-117

Activity Directions: Review how career planning is like reading a mall directory to your employees, based on pages 109-110. List how you will describe this concept to your employees including the analogy of the manager as a "mall directory" when it comes to career planning:

_____

_____

_____

Pick at least two of your employees and hold career discussions. You may wish to create a diagram similar to the example in Activity 7.3. Discussion flow suggestion:
1. Describe the mall directory example (pages 109-110).
2. Ask the employee about his/her short- and long-term career plans.
3. Discuss where the employee is now. Ask the person what skills and abilities they currently have that would make their career choice possible.
4. Ask what additional training or skills they would like to develop to prepare for the future.

Results of your discussion with employee One:

_____

_____

_____

_____

Results of your discussion with employee Two:

_____

_____

_____

_____

Activity 7.5
Brainstorm Skill Development
The Management Map II reference pages 118-119

Activity Directions: There is a new definition for development. Development doesn't have to mean a training class. Review the leadership development example on pages 118-119. Brainstorm creative ideas for the following three skill development needs.

1. Brainstorm development ideas to improve **time management** skills:

_____

_____

_____

_____

2. Brainstorm development ideas to improve **presentation** skills:

_____

_____

_____

_____

3. Brainstorm development ideas to improve **project management** skills:

_____

_____

_____

_____

Example: Leadership development

• Read book on leadership	• Lead a project team at work
• Watch videos on leadership	• Interview leaders about leadership
• Read articles on leadership	• Volunteer as community leader
• Create a report with insights from any of the above	• Locate a leadership mentor

EIGHT

THE ROAD TO EXCELLENCE
Managing Employee Performance

Items to Collect for This Chapter's Activities:
☐ Process instructions on performance reviews for your company
☐ Copies of forms used for performance appraisals

Chapter Learning Points:
- Evaluate team member performance
- Create positive performance improvement plans

***The Management Map II* reference pages:** 125-140

Chapter Summary:
The chapter begins with a discussion on keeping employees on the right path to avoid paying the "price of delay" by postponing feedback and clarifying expectations.

High achievement managers lead highly motivated team members who are committed and engaged. High achieving managers focus on goal accomplishment by establishing expectations, setting high but achievable goals, coaching and giving feedback, and removing barriers to success.

Every company has its own method of reviewing employee performance, however they typically all share the following process: 1) Establish goals and expectations. 2) Observe, track progress and capture data. 3) Provide ongoing coaching and direction. 4) Complete your company's forms. 5) Discuss the performance review. The chapter then provides insights, examples, and information on how to complete these five performance review activities.

Your Initial Reflection:
What did you like best about the chapter? What topic resonated with you?

_____

_____

_____

Which concepts in the chapter apply to your department or organization?

_____

_____

_____

Which quote did you like from the chapter?

_____

_____

_____

Journey Progress — Check after you complete each activity:

☐ **Activity 8.1: Performance Management Process** — Gather and review your organization's review process and forms.

☐ **Activity 8.2: Examples by Rating Category** — Write behavioral expectations by performance rating and appraisal categories.

☐ **Activity 8.3: Tracking Performance Data** — Determine which performance data to track and how you will track it for inclusion on appraisal forms.

☐ **Activity 8.4: Appraisal Feedback Comments** — Practice writing appraisal feedback comments and receiving feedback.

Activity 8.1
Performance Management Process
The Management Map II reference pages 128-132

Activity Directions: This is your opportunity to explore your company's performance management form and process. Gather the forms and procedure guides for your organization to respond to the following questions.

1. Does your organization have a performance management form? Create a place on your computer to be able to easily locate the form.

_____

_____

2. Are there rating levels such a 1-5? How many rating levels are there? List them here:

_____

_____

_____

3. Does your form have performance categories such as quality and quantity? List all categories here:

_____

_____

_____

4. Are there specific instructions for managers regarding how and when to complete the process? Where are they located? Add a summary of key instructions here:

_____

_____

_____

5. Does your organization utilize a self-appraisal form? Add it to the folder with your appraisal form.

_____

_____

Activity 8.2

Examples by Rating Category

The Management Map II **reference pages 131-132**

Activity Directions: In this activity you will list observable behaviors in three performance levels in the chart below: above expectations, meets expectations, and below expectations. Your company may use more or fewer performance levels. By writing descriptive performance examples, it will assist you in evaluating performance consistently against a standard and also provide your employees with a clear understanding of what is expected. Three typical evaluation categories—quality, productivity, and teamwork—are listed with space for you to add two more areas relevant to your organization. Be as descriptive as possible as you list what performance "looks like" in each rating category.

(See example on teamwork located on page 132 to assist you in completing this table.)

	Above Expectations	Meets Expectations	Below Expectations
Quality			
Productivity			
Teamwork			

Activity 8.3
Tracking Performance Data
The Management Map II **reference pages 132-133**

Activity Directions: Reviews are more accurate and easier to complete if a tracking mechanism is used to capture significant events and data. Examine your organization's review form. Determine the type of information you would like to track to make your reviews more accurate and completion of the form easier. You can use the examples in the book or make up your own. (See other examples on page 132.)

Chart 1: Data/information you are currently tracking:

Type of Information	How to Track	Information Location
Example: Quantity of calls answered	Download statistics on a spreadsheet	Company intranet, save to an Excel file

Chart 2: Data/information you would like to add to your tracking routine:

Type of Information	How to Track	Information Location

Activity 8.4

Appraisal Feedback Comments

The Management Map II reference pages 133-136

Activity Directions: For performance feedback comments to be effective, they must be objective and not subjective. Comments must also be clear, specific, business focused, self-esteem focused, and non-discriminatory. Write one or two performance feedback comments below and obtain feedback from a peer based on the criteria in the chart at the bottom of the page. If time allows, practice saying your written comment with a partner to get feedback.

a) Title:	b) Rating Category
Performance review comment:	

Feedback Chart	Excellent	Good Job	Needs Work
Comment was objective not subjective			
Comment was clear			
Comment was specific			
Comment was business focused			
Comment was self-esteemed focused			
Comment was non-discriminatory			

Additional Feedback Comments:

NINE

TURBULENCE AHEAD...
Navigating Challenging Situations

Items to Collect for This Chapter's Activities:
❑ Your company's process for coaching and disciplinary action
❑ Forms required by your company for documenting corrective performance discussions

Chapter Learning Points:

* Use experience for challenging situations
* Take action when coaching isn't enough

The Management Map II **reference pages:** 141-157

Chapter Summary:
The chapter discusses how experienced managers handle challenging people situations. The phrase "stop it before it sticks" reminds experienced managers to solve performance problems early. A three-step process was introduced in this chapter with three reflective questions: 1) What specifically is the team member doing? 2) Does the behavior matter? 3) What can you do to support a change in behavior?

When coaching and feedback do not correct the situation, it is time to begin your company's discipline process. The root word of discipline means "to teach." By focusing on a mindset of "teaching," the disciplinary process can be positive and constructive. It is important to review your company's corrective process including any forms, procedures, or approvals required. Your company may refer to the corrective process as a performance improvement plan.

Before starting your process it is important to thoroughly investigate the situation, giving the employee the benefit of the doubt and not jumping to conclusions. After the investigation, the following discussion steps were recommended: 1) Provide the facts, 2) Probe and listen, 3) Discuss process, and 4) Create required documentation.

Your Initial Reflection:
What did you like best about the chapter? What topic resonated with you?

_____

_____

_____

Which concepts in the chapter apply to your department or organization?

_____

_____

_____

Which quote did you like from the chapter?

_____

_____

_____

Journey Progress — Check after you complete each activity:

❏ **Activity 9.1: Consequence of Labeling** — Discuss negative labels and their consequences.

❏ **Activity 9.2: Stop It Before It Sticks** — Analyze a situation where you will need to provide feedback and coaching.

❏ **Activity 9.3: Conduct a Disciplinary Discussion** — Practice conducting a disciplinary discussion and documentation according to your company's forms and guidelines.

❏ **Activity 9.4: Strategies for Handling Difficult Situations** — Brainstorm challenging situations and then match strategies to the situation.

Activity 9.1

Consequence of Labeling

The Management Map II **reference pages 141-146**

Activity Directions: In the first column, brainstorm labels you've heard about employees. In the second column indicate the negative consequences of these labels to careers and reputation

Labels	Negative Consequences of Labeling
Example: Troublemaker	The employee will have a difficult time being promoted with this label and others will search to find occurrences of "trouble" behavior.

What can you do as a manager to prevent your employees being labeled?

_____

_____

_____

_____

Activity 9.2

Stop It Before It Sticks

The Management Map II reference pages 142-146

Activity Directions: Think about a situation where you feel the need to provide feedback to a team member before the behavior becomes ingrained and more difficult to change. See the example provided on pages 145-146 as you respond to the following:

1. What specifically is the team member doing? Describe the objective facts based on what you have seen or heard.

    _____

    _____

    _____

    _____

2. Does the behavior matter? If yes, describe the long-term impact to the organization and employee.

    _____

    _____

    _____

    _____

3. What can you do to support a change in behavior? List ideas but also plan a question to ask that would engage the employee in contributing ideas to correct the situation.

    _____

    _____

    _____

    _____

If time allows, practice saying your prepared comments out loud with a partner and ask for feedback.

Activity 9.3
Conduct a Disciplinary Discussion
The Management Map II **reference pages 146-155**

Activity Directions: In this activity you will roleplay a mock corrective discussion with another manager, playing your employee. Start by describing the situation and then follow the action steps based on the example on pages 152-153. Make notes on what you will say for each step during your practice. After your practice, ask your partner to roleplay with you and provide feedback.

Describe the situation, including previous feedback discussions:

_____

_____

Step 1: Provide the facts

_____

_____

_____

_____

Step 2: Probe and listen

_____

_____

_____

_____

Step 3: Discuss process

_____

_____

_____

_____

Step 4: Create required documentation (complete your company form)

_____

_____

For additional coaching, discuss Activity 9.3 with your managers or human resource professionals to gain their input.

Activity 9.4
Strategies for Handling Difficult Situations
The Management Map II reference pages 153-155

Activity Directions: Despite all your research and pre-planning for the disciplinary discussion, situations may arise that will present a challenge. Brainstorm situations that have developed or statements employees have made during disciplinary discussions that you have found difficult in the right column. An example is provided.

Strategy	Difficult Situations
B	Employee starts to cry during the discussion

Activity Directions continued: Review the strategies below and match the letter to the situations brainstormed above in the left column.

A. **Referral to Resources** – If you suspect the causes of the problem are employee or family personal problems, ask human resources for available community referral resources. The employee may be eligible for company benefit assistance. They also might be aware of other community resources available. Managers are not in a position to offer counseling of a personal nature, which should always be conducted by a trained professional. By referring the employee to the other resources to handle their personal issues, you can then remain focused on the business issues.

B. **Conducting the Discussion in Two Sessions** – Occasionally the employee is not emotionally prepared to participate in an effective problem-solving session. This reaction could be due to being surprised by the problem or just someone who typically exhibits a strong emotional response to corrective action discussions. If you feel a more productive problem-solving session could be held if delayed, set a date and time **ASAP** (as soon as possible), indicating to the employee the need to be prepared to discuss the issues and solutions at that time.

Activity 9.4 Continued

C. **Investigate the Situation Further** – Facts may surface during the discussion about which you were previously unaware. If the employee tells you about additional facts or situations it is best to give him/her the benefit of the doubt, investigate further, and set another date to continue the discussion. Involve your manager or a member of human resources if you need assistance in investigating all the facts. It is always best to be thorough than to have to retract a disciplinary notice because all the facts weren't investigated first.

D. **Ask for Coaching or a Practice Session** – If you anticipate the disciplinary session will be challenging or that issues may be discussed which make you feel concerned, utilize the expertise of your manager or the human resources department. They will be able to prepare you with coaching tips and even help you practice your responses. If you feel the discussion will be really volatile, someone could also participate with you during the discussion. After a disciplinary session, if you have a concern that the discussion was unproductive or if the employee has made a complaint that they have not been treated fairly, report it to your manager or human resources.

E. **Maintain Your Composure** – Occasionally managers may feel defensive if their attempts to correct a problem are met with arguments, justification, or accusations. Practicing maintaining your composure and keeping focused on the issues will keep you from becoming defensive. Don't let anyone push your "hot buttons" with the purpose of derailing you from conducting an effective discussion. Keep focused on the six-step process.

TEN

RECALCULATING...
Continuous Improvement on Your Management Journey

Items to Collect for This Chapter's Activities:
❑ Information about your organization's quality programs
❑ Instructions and a diagram of a process flow analysis

Chapter Learning Points:

- Create a continuous improvement culture
- Apply the spirit of continuous improvement to your management journey

The Management Map II **reference pages:** 159-171

Chapter Summary:

Citius, altius, fortius... the Olympic motto, which means faster, higher, stronger. This chapter begins with a discussion of how this theme can inspire team members to perform at the best of their abilities in the spirit of continuous improvement.

It is important to know and utilize your organization's quality initiative program and the various continuous improvement tools. Three tools were presented in this chapter: Plus/Delta, process flow analysis, and Work-Out.

The chapter concludes with a discussion on how to continuously improve your own skills as a manager. The first of the two methods presented is self-reflection and a four-step method on how to analyze your strengths and challenges. The second method is via a 360 review to obtain feedback from your manager, peers, and direct reports.

Your Initial Reflection:
What did you like best about the chapter? What topic resonated with you?

_____

_____

_____

Which concepts in the chapter apply to your department or organization?

_____

_____

_____

Which quote did you like from the chapter?

_____

_____

_____

Journey Progress — Check after you complete each activity:

❏ **Activity 10.1: Examine Your Quality Program** — Research the quality program in your organization.

❏ **Activity 10.2: Facilitate a Plus/Delta Session** — Pick a time and topic to hold a Plus/Delta session with your team.

❏ **Activity 10.3: Process Flow Analysis** — Pick a process that could be improved and lead your team in a process flow analysis.

❏ **Activity 10.4: Self-Reflection Activity** — Go through the four steps of continuous improvement reflection.

❏ **Activity 10.5: Optional: Complete a 360 Assessment** — Request a 360 assessment and then reflect on feedback.

Activity 10.1
Examine Your Quality Program
The Management Map II reference pages 160-161

Activity Directions: Many organizations have a continuous improvement/quality program. It might be known as Total Quality Management, Lean Manufacturing, Six Sigma, Kaizen, etc. Investigate and learn your organization's program by responding to the following questions:

1. Does your organization's quality program have a name? What is it?

_____

_____

2. Is there an individual or department responsible for quality in your organization? List names and contact information here.

_____

_____

3. What tools, techniques, or processes are available to teach your team members quality improvement? (You may wish to visit with the person responsible for quality in your department to learn about availability of resources.)

_____

_____

_____

_____

4. List one quality tool, technique, and/or process you located and how you will use it with your team.

_____

_____

_____

_____

Activity 10.2
Facilitate a Plus/Delta Session
The Management Map II **reference pages 161-162**

Activity Directions: Pick a time and topic and meet with your team to hold a Plus/Delta session. Decide whether you will use the flip chart method or self-stick notes process. Begin with a definition and explanation of the Plus/Delta method on page 161. After the session, reflect on what you learned about the process in question 2 listed below.

1. **Topic for your Plus/Delta meeting** (examples: work produced at the end of the week, a special project, after a "busy season," etc.):

   _____

   _____

   _____

Plus + (What went well)	Delta △(Ideas for the future)

2. What did you learn from your Plus/Delta session? How will you change the process in the future?

   _____

   _____

   _____

Activity 10.3
Process Flow Analysis
The Management Map II reference pages 162-163

Activity Directions: Determine if your organization can assist you with training tools on process flow analysis. If they don't have information, a quick internet search or a YouTube video can supply you with the basic concept. Also, re-read the description on pages 162-163. Decide on a process that needs to be improved and gather everyone associated with that process for a working session. Have a flip chart and markers available. After the session, complete questions 3 and 4.

1. Choose a process to analyze, being clear in the description you will give to attendees and the objectives of the session. List process to be analyzed:

_____

_____

_____

_____

2. Provide everyone with process flow analysis information, tools, and examples.

_____

_____

3. What did you learn from the process flow analysis you conducted? How will you change the process in the future?

_____

_____

_____

_____

4. What other quality tools do you plan to use in the future?

_____

_____

_____

Activity 10.4
Self-Reflection Activity
The Management Map II reference pages 166-168

Activity Directions: Experienced managers know they should focus on continuous improvement for themselves and embrace self-reflection and development. Use the following reflective questions to reflect on your skills.

Step I: Think about activities or projects where you have really excelled. What types of skills were used in these activities? List them here:

_____

_____

Step II: Review the strengths you listed in Step I.

1. How can you use these strengths more in your current role? In a future role?

_____

_____

2. Will you have to tone down your strengths or use them less often in a future role?

_____

_____

Step III: Think about activities or projects that didn't go so well. What type of skills were required that were not your natural strengths? List them here:

_____

_____

Step IV: Review the skills identified in Step III.

1. Will you need to use these skills more or less when you advance to your next opportunity?

_____

_____

2. If you will need to use these skills more frequently in the future, list a development plan.

_____

_____

Activity 10.5
Optional: Complete a 360 Assessment
The Management Map II **reference pages 168-170**

Activity Directions: A 360 assessment is a process to obtain feedback from the people who work around you. This usually includes your manager, peers, and direct reports. Meet with your manager or a member of human resources to learn if a 360 process is available and if so, schedule it. After receiving your 360 feedback, reflect on the following questions:

1. What surprised you about your feedback? What didn't surprise you?

_____

_____

_____

_____

2. What strengths were identified in your feedback? How can you utilize your strengths more in your current role?

_____

_____

_____

_____

3. What development areas were identified and how will you develop?

_____

_____

_____

_____

Final Activity
Action Plan

Activity Directions: Flip through *The Management Map II Companion Workbook* to review all the concepts we discussed. Identify three key concepts. Develop your plan of action for implementing your identified key concepts.

1. Key Concept: _____

Chapter Title: _____

Specific actions I will take: _____

_____

_____

_____

2. Key Concept: _____

Chapter Title: _____

Specific actions I will take: _____

_____

_____

_____

3. Key Concept: _____

Chapter Title: _____

Specific actions I will take: _____

_____

_____

_____

RESOURCES FOR YOUR MANAGEMENT JOURNEY

Management Skills Resource, **Inc**. is your resource for all your management development training needs. Our products and services are dedicated to the advancement and on-the-job application of effective management principles.

Building the *competence*, *confidence*, and *courage* of your management teams through:

Classroom Training — Using proven templates, we custom design workshops based on your company's culture, policies, and procedures.

Training Products — Our training products and learning assessment are always designed to align people's skills and behavior with organizational strategies.

Management Skills Resource, Inc.

www.ManagementSkillsResource.com
Info@ManagementSkillsResource.com

About the Author

Deborah Avrin, MS, SPHR, brings over 20 years of human resources and training experience to her company, Management Skills Resource, Inc. Her coaching skills have assisted countless managers to improve their performance in such diverse industries as financial services, manufacturing, utilities, transportation, education, non-profit, and telecommunications.

Prior to beginning her consulting practice in 1998, Deborah Avrin held a variety of top-level human resources leadership positions in both the financial services and manufacturing industries. She also has held operational management positions, which enables her to understand the unique training needs of managers. Her reputation is as a motivator, with an inspiring training style that encourages others to excel.

Her company, Management Skills Resource, Inc., works with organizations that want to build the confidence, competence, and courage of their management teams through creative training workshops.

Her educational background includes a BBA in human resources and a MS degree in organizational behavior. Deborah Avrin also holds a lifetime Senior Professional in Human Resources (SPHR) certification.